THE DESCENT OF HEAVEN
OVER THE LAKE

Sheryl Noethe

Sheryl Noethe

THE DESCENT OF HEAVEN
OVER THE LAKE

with graphics by

Charles Thompson Taylor

Minnesota Voices Project #21

New Rivers Press 1984

Grateful acknowledgement is offered to the editors of the following publications where some of the poems in this book first appeared: *Christian Science Monitor*, *City Pages*, *Great River Review*, *Lake Street Review*, *Ohio Review*, *Red Tape Magazine*, and *Twenty-Five Minnesota Poets* (anthology).

The Descent Of Heaven Over The Lake has been published with the aid of grants from the Jerome Foundation, the Dayton Hudson Foundation (with funds provided by B. Dalton, Bookseller), the Metropolitan Regional Arts Council (with funds appropriated by the Minnesota State Legislature), the First Bank System Foundation, and the United Arts Fund (with funds provided in part by the McKnight Foundation).

New Rivers Press books are distributed by:

Small Press Distribution, Inc.
1784 Shattuck Ave.
Berkeley, CA 94709

Bookslinger
213 East 4th St.
St. Paul, MN 55101

The Descent of Heaven Over The Lake has been manufactured in the United States of America for New Rivers Press, Inc. (C. W. Truesdale, editor/publisher), 1602 Selby Ave., St. Paul, MN 55104 in a first edition of 1000 copies.

For Arlene Griller

And For Richard Schiff

THE DESCENT OF HEAVEN
OVER THE LAKE

THE DESCENT OF HEAVEN
OVER THE LAKE

I

Y.S. JEREZ

She told me that she loved me today
before I took out my canoe.
She had a dream of the largest pearl,
hidden away, growing for me in the
belly of the constant dark, in the
oyster, in the deepest waters.

I used to take her to the pyramids
and once when she climbed too high
the wind almost took her away from
me and into the ruins. She fought
the pleats of a cotton skirt that
blew up into her face, she swayed
and my head reeled at the idea,
the loss of her.

When I go diving I come home
with giant lobsters and she
cracks the shell, with a hammer,
tears the meat away from them.
When she licks the juice from
her hands my heart goes harder.

I carry the canoe on my shoulders
and slide it into the water. It is
common to die out here and never
be found. But I will wash in with
the tide all the way to her hammock
in my final attempt to bring beauty
to her life; clenched in each dead
hand I am bringing her pearls.

MR. BOVARY

When you are brooding beneath
the dark green branches,
waiting silently for me
in the corner chair,
blue and sulky as the
thick curtains that
you have pushed shut
against the afternoon,

when you are pretending
to sleep, face pale as
the pillow, watching me
from one cracked green eye
as I slide past in a peach robe,

your mood is as dense as
the stilted air. And I
brush against you, desiring
to fit as close as milk
to the sides of a bowl,
shatter your calm,
spill you all over my arms and hands,
and I break you open
like a blue jar
of ether.

JOSEF

I would place you in a Rousseau painting,
green bamboo stalks and plants like genitalia
glistening in the midst of your jungles.

The family drives to the edge of the
clearing and forces the child out
of the back of the car. They drive
off and he looks for a tree to climb.

I would dress you in bone rings and ash.
I would watch you stand in the sun
with flies around your head and the
plumage of a flower-like bird
covering your sex.

I would place you in a village of
cannibals who play at growing sugar cane.
They would be a festive people, they would
dance the skin off your feet. How you will
tremble when the drums start up, how you
will laugh in your throat waiting for
your turn in the circle, one of the
young bachelors, soon to leave for
another village, seeking a wife.
Over the hills are a people of
your mother's kin. Soon you
will take your old waterskin
and drape it across your
scarred chest. Soon you
will walk out into the
land of zebra and the
crouching hyena.
Soon, too soon,
Lost to me.

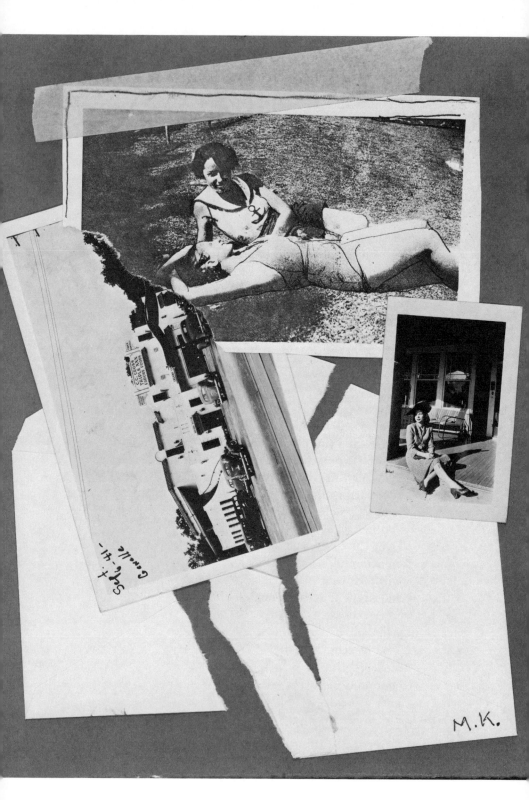

POEM FOR MARY KARR

I get the cold letter that describes
the end of the magic dance. At first
I have to laugh, how the words move
faster than a pulse in disarray,
the gasps of a great horse, how
thick life has got.

I read the letter again. This heat.
The sun. I lay it down and lean
against the white enamel stove.

You were naked beneath a parasol
watching from the beach as I
walked into the water, that
summer I taught you how to swim.

Rolling in July's delirious sleep
I hear the wind chimes start ringing
as people come up to the house with
torches. I am tearing your poems
from the walls when I am taken with
the illusion of burning. The people
outside dream that they are laughing.
Standing on a ledge outside the window
I dream that you no longer care.
They call for me to jump down to them.

Let's go back to the beach together.
somewhat sober, too hot to touch
without blistering. Let us go back
and dip into the water from a wooden
boat, our heads shaved, skin oiled,
gathering sponges and fans to sell along the road.

We could go back to the bar as strangers,
our hair tucked into our hats. You could
turn down the drink I'd send you, shaking

your head and turning away.
Let us go back to the beach and the bar
and my house together. We could just lay
exhausted upon the sheets, making no wrinkles,
no signs, simply the talcum of your hair
leaving its scent on the pillow. We'll
leave behind our silk shirts and mysteries
and walk back down to the water.

On the way to work it starts raining.
A woman gets on the bus who looks like you,
her hair's all wrong, and her eyes aren't
nearly as dark as yours,
no matter. My mouth fills with blood.
Fight enough dragon, become dragon.

3 METAPHORS FOR LOVE

A man steps from a bar out onto the street
shaking his head and waving a gun.
His friend weaves uncertainly behind him,
holding out a hand .
The sun poisons his liquor through his head.

The body is struck like a bell and makes
no sound. Stopped ringing long ago, it seems.
"Look," you say, "I'm beginning to leave you."
The trees burst into flame. You try
to stay asleep.

An old woman on a boat bites into a lemon.
Your body rings and you taste her joy as
her teeth break the skin. The ferry breaks
neatly into the waves of the sea. A soldier
walks by and offers you a cigarette.
His grin breaks into your gaze.
You look past him, towards the sea,
where you'd hoped the dolphins might be.

WHY DID YOU SAY

When the pale faces of the town children
peered into the garden I was hidden
behind vine and screen. Waiting,
I suppose, for what I know now was
untrue. I kept myself behind the
thick growth of morning glory
against the shuttered window.

It seems impossible to
brush my hair or pick up the
dishes that hardened with old
meals in the same way that you
have hardened towards me.
Had I gone crazy you would
never have known, zipping
away south on a lark.

Years later your glance
would suggest that life,
and what I learned before
I left it and took a new name.

Since you
I have been to Tetuan, Cueta, Algeciras,
and I have been to the disco with
spanish furniture salesmen.
I miss them no more than I miss you.
I have seen the marketplace of
Laroche, the superstitions of Azhila.

Often I wondered about ever getting
home again. Not once did I consider
you. Danger co-opted memory.
I strode across big sky and
salt lake, through sleeping eye
black earth, willow, olive and lemon.
I lived for a while as a farmer's wife,

and had a much larger garden than ever,
big enough to hide the smaller children
who were only given away by the birds
dragging broken-looking wings away
from the nest.

I sent you postcards from Madrid,
saying, "Watteau makes me remember."
That same afternoon a busboy at
cafeteria el prado made rolling eyes
and did a greasy walk behind the counter.
He kept me enthralled for too long.
I escaped into the rain, a Spain full
of umbrellas, oranges, gypsies
carrying baskets of groceries
in baskets on their heads.

I waited, fruitlessly, once
in a room but I have been away,
come back, found you,
and this not caring makes the journey complete.

SYLVIA

Sometimes I try to remember
what it was like to love you.
There's a snapshot, somewhere,
your face a dark blur above
a white suit. I am holding
a flower of some sort, dressed
in chiffon. I had not thought
of any of this yet.

Two years later and I
am holding a child.
You pose next to your car.
I carry a look of concern.
The child watches like a referee.
A math whiz, compounding our
mistakes. You look like
you could use a drink.

The pictures are jumbled into
a drawer. We can't hold on to
happiness or each other.
Your gaze goes over my shoulder.
I shout in a language that
doesn't translate. A child
throws things at mirrors.

You dream about the princess
of Sweden. I contemplate religion,
a career. Our girl pretends we're
dead, or cowards. Worse is her
face when we fight. "Mama," she says,
"why don't you run away?"
If I said, "love," she'd laugh at me.
So I say tired.
I say afraid.

MUNDO

Our affair is with the earth.
    The mother
you work with every day.
    And nights
the field calls to you
    in your bed.

You dream that you are
    a bee
your thighs brush
    rose hips
you move from pistil to stamen
    purring,
hunkering up to those petals.

Something yellow from the
    center
of the blossom has gathered
    on you
heady with delight you do a
    little dance
for the rest of the hive.

Someone comes to collect your
    pollen,
empty your baskets, you forget
    yourself
and hum something from the club
    Blue Moon.

By now all the other bees have
    memorized
your dance and bodies like hot
    silver
they're off in the sun and the
    flowers

are whistling, "Hey, honey,
over here!"

You sober up. It's summer. You're a saxaphone.
You wait for the next dancer to come
        staggering
home.

CALL IT COINCIDENCE

At the dinner party they turn to abortion.
A design like roses on the white tablecloth
where the wine could be blood. You stand for
a while behind a door where the room is filled
with poinsetta, amaryllis, hibiscus, azealea—you understand.
Everything is red. Your hands. The drops on your shoes.
You have made your world incarnadine.
Flesh-colored, from the inside.

What you can do is this—imagine
it's a desert, a room on the desert
filled with buckets of sand. Think
of cacti and grit, think barren, barren, dry.

It's impossible for you to get back to the city.
You stay at a house on the St. Croix. Borrow a
white nightgown. A featherbed. More wine, red.
There's a thunderstorm in February, lightning.
All night you hear the hissing rain.

Dawn comes you wrestle hors d' oeuvres
away from the cat, walk down to the water
and wreck your shoes. Driving home you aim
yourself back at your life but dazed by
events and this single release you make
blurry landings, miss your mark, and stand
damp, dizzy, shoeless, on the wrong side of
where it is, precisely, you wanted to be.

S FROM S

The moon was full and white as an egg or ice
    illuminating the sky the way
god lights up the bodies of his blessed.
    I could feel the desire you spoke of
make itself real in the chattering of
    my teeth and trembling limbs—
you spoke of the cold, I wanted to stay
    with desire. That word, pointed to in
my poems, and the finger touching at the
    top of my spine, the room at the top
of your house where all night I asked you
    —What is that sound, you said,—only water.
I knelt knee-deep in the dream handing you
    agates, pulling them from the beach and
into my mouth.
    I made them shine for you, bright as fire.
I heard crackling, smelled flame, the heat
    of your body, I couldn't breathe.
—There's no fire, you said, It's only water.

We were lit in the full moon
    in the pointed edge of an attic
visible to the entire sleeping city.
    This window, lit like a spotlight
in the shine. Only a dog awake,
    and howling, raising his muzzle to
us and to the moon, wanting to understand
    this sound coming out of him all on its own.

WHAT YOU HOLD

You're sustenance farming in the french twilight
and what Monet saw is what you see, is yours,
save your onions which are bigger than any field of lilies,
better than the gardens that sway and feed no one.

There is no romance at dusk. Just time to chase
home the herd. The black bread in your pocket is life,
and the man at the easel is missing the point.

When you sit down and bite into the bread
you are pleasing your god and his anger dwindles.
He gives you a child, and he lets it grow fat.

THIS, MUCH LATER

End of summer. Nights you can smell the transition
to fall, mornings are cold as the approaching autumn.
I sleep with a blanket and rise in a thick wool robe,
bundling myself into the grey start of day.

These letters that tell of the changing season,
they're spaced so closely, just last week
I described for you the snowfall, and
yesterday I sweltered at ballet. As we age
time hastens and there is a poignancy to
each reflective dawn.

Last night I drank a little moselblumchen
and it lingered in my throat, suggesting
nectarines and plums on steep hillsides,
I thought of the mist off the river,
the rows of delicate grapevines, and
I thought of you.

Dear friend, make yourself happy.
My hands hesitate as I write,
tremble for you, for us, for
the cool garden boy asleep in my bed.

I love him like I once loved you,
and this passion has never left me. .
Clasped in the circle of
arms, legs, and enchanted
we run down the horizon.
Tangled in his youth
I envision you precisely.
Gone now for so long, so far away,
no longer mine.

J.B., LATER STILL

When we are finished speaking on the phone
broken glass runs in thin splinters from
my nipples to my heart. A gorilla is
pounding a drum in my pants.

I imagine myself at the wedding of you
and the heiress. I see myself on my knees
in the garden. I see myself drinking
away the years with red wine.
A lush pink tulip limp with heat.

Approaching anesthesis like the
hallway to a long monastery where
the monk who leads me minds nothing.
Not my sin, not my penance.
We move on our knees up to the altar.
There is not enough blood on the tiles
to atone for my old life, or for this
anticipation of more. I crawl harder.

The heavy flowers have fallen out
of their wineglass simply by leaning.
I expect I'll pass out at your reception,
slipping onto the lawn of the church
in my strapless black gown.

Deposed. Autumnal.

II

STORY

I was a soldier, then, who wanted
nothing so much as to curl up in
my mother's arms, except maybe to eat.

This was that village where they hid
their vegetables beneath the dirt floors
of their houses, beneath pig sties, &

in their daughter's beds. I boiled
water anyway, and went house to house
holding out my hand.

I told them I would add the most
important part, the heart of our
meal. Slowly they brought me
a carrot, an onion, and a bone.

I threw my stone into the soup.

2.

This is how the affair went.
Your refusal rolling into my bowl.
A yellow ball of poison.
Inedible. Jaw-breaking. Mis-represented.

THE BOXER, DUK-KOO KIM, COLLAPSED

A canceled flight, angel
revoked. It appears that
he is listening to himself,
the whisper, the blood in
his brain, the vein that
tore like paper.
He lays on the mat and
the crowd waits.

He drops his guard.
The unknown soldier roams
the vast damp. He frowns,
a little, trying to catch
that last sound, that roar,
the smell of rubber as his
head, or something, thumps
the mat. All the metal stars
and heat. He went down saying
"What," or "Wait." Just like
that. You can see how carefully
he waves goodbye.

Meanwhile a saint in India
discards his body like a
playing card. He intercepts
the dying boxer and takes
his hand. He holds their
arms over their heads
like champions.

BLEECKER STREET, WITH AN "A"

I found a job in the garment district
in the dreamfactory
the other girls whistle like birds.

On our lunch break we lay on cots
and trill, inventing the men we'll meet.

And talk about the moon together,
because you couldn't say blood,
that tidal thing.

Our misery snags like fingernails
in the long lines of cotton going
under the wheels of our arms,

Fabric billowing in the waves
of our departure.

Fire escapes like lace
on the buildings, we wouldn't
reach, never got to, as
all our dreams went up in smoke.

SUMMER, 1983

Every night my father comes into the cat and guest bedroom, stands over me and says Night Toots and I say, Daddy, got a cigarette, struggle awake and sit up in my army shirt and he lights one up and says, Put it out before you go to sleep now.

When he slides from beneath a bashed ford on his creeper his hair is as wild as a rooster's, he wipes his hand on his pants and holds it out to all of my friends.

There is a cougar in the back yard, a pontiac in the garage and two old fords in front of the house. His garage is an old parts place jammed with tools, oil-soaked dirt floor,

where he goes out back, hunts around and returns with a radiator he's had since the sixties he turns it around in his hand and says, "That'll be six bucks."

My dad and his brothers have lived in the bellies of cars for some thirty years. They stand around and rev up cars with perpetual concern and black fingers.

When he sleeps I hear each breath like something he's pulling from deep out of a swamp. When I was very young he always took me with him, holding his arm out across my chest.

He raced in an old highway patrol car, with a 427 under the hood, and I stood next to him grin widened by velocity. We left Duane and Ben in the dust, I smiled from ear to ringing ear.

Aunts Leona and Trionne asked why did a girl want to go with the men? The answer was simple: speed. Fear of holding still forever. I wanted my head tugged back by the wind, the wind caught in my chest.

We raced from Lake Benton to Balaton and through Gaylord and Sleepy Eye, passing the station where Eddie worked until he stood straight up, going eighty, on his Honda through Cross Corners.

Everybody knew the Noethe boys. Jim boxed Golden Gloves. Tommy had dark hair as polished as a slipper and Ben the face that women wanted to return to.

They fought together outside of bars and put together cars in a backyard where the grass grew high as wheat, hiding bathtubs and fins and broken windshields as old cars gave up their innards.

Younger, faster men are not so lucky. My brother's car is winched to a telephone pole and then backed up until the front end uncrumples. They tear out the fans and hoses and cruise junkyards for parts.

My father lays the front quarter panel and the hood and grill across wooden horses and pounds them back into sheets of uninterrupted metal. He fits them back on the car and it's ready,

for whiskey, low bridges and foreign suburbs, waiting for my middle brother who barrels through like a bat from hell.

NOT EVEN ENNUI

When I leave the house
I hear you scolding yourself.
You are looking through the
poems and do not find them
beautiful. You live in a small
room at the top of yourself,
like an attic.
Each time you make the climb
expecting to find the hidden
trunk that no one else has
ever opened. You life the lid
and are obscured by smells
from the past. You put back
your face like a dog who's
caught scent of something,
those slow-running chickens
on a neighbor's farm.
Big clumsy sheep where blood
pulses behind the wool.
Sharp as you are,
you'll reach it.

When I come home
you are holding crumpled papers
and you say, "Junk."
I think of a boat big enough
to live on, and then I think
of what goes in the arm and
sails from vein to heart.

You do not mean Hong Kong
or heroin. You mean that
you have promised yourself
a life of words. And I come
home to your Sour Look.
An absence that is here
everyday. What word is it

that you keep waking up without.

If I could bloom with language
like other women look
handsome in their silk suits,
if I could turn to you
with lips like a fuschia
at the collarbone, a soap dish
above the heart, & orchids
behind my every mouth like
other women with their
lovely faces, then I
could be sure to keep
your sulky gaze on me.
Not even ennui could distract you.

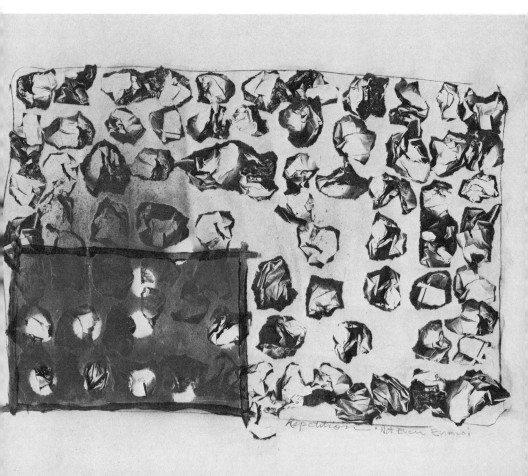

REPETITION

You ask in your letter
if I've seen the sky.
Night, one thousand
times night, I see
the sky. Black moons following white.

It's snowing. I won't sleep tonight.
Seeking oblivion, lifelike, almost
love but not quite.

Outside it's all white, divine,
but divine is a word, like desire,
that you are said to use too often.

Loosely, like a slack rope on a
horse, but Horse, that's forbidden
you too, and besides, it means
heroin and whether it's on your
knees in somebody's kitchen or
using the color blue in a poem
one more time,
it's bad style to repeat yourself.

And style is what they remember.
They'll say you began imitating
yourself. They'll say "habit."
Your sweet mouth soured.
You kept finding new ways to
use Horse. You ran away, brown
eyes, long legs, and a big heart.

But boy, you act like nothing
matters, like it's all water,
and when I tried to talk to you,
winter hazing the city outside
the piano bar, you only stared
at your hands and said, "let's run."

I think I should've spoken
more fiercely, held you by
your hair, pushing words into
you, jagged words that tear
your throat when you swallow them.

THE GOOSE GIRL

The peacocks seem to scream all night.
I no longer hear them.
The spotted cow that wanders
has dropper her calf, as far
west as the fence allows.
We rejoice. She looks back
at him with quiet certainty.

Everything here is new & slippery,
tight as a green bud and innocent
beneath a steady rain. The Mystery
does not evaporate. It is as solid
as coal, as dense. It reappears
in a glittering disguise, from deep
in the molten fist, from the red core
that buckles in what is the guts of the
planet. It is made precious.
It returns on the forehead of the
black calf, a perfect white diamond.

I went out to feed the swan.
The postman brought your letter.
as empty envelope, and a note,
"Everything enclosed."
Did you forget?
Is this a joke?
I am simple. I raise ducks.
Please explain. Is this
how you say we are finished?

And from so far away and from
all on your own. I could understand
a wife who hears the same complaint
one hundred times. Or people who
lay like strangers until one
of them slips out to torch the house,
people who lay on each other like

dogs on the manger, unable to eat
straw but snarling when anyone
with an appetite approaches.

But when is hunger not desire?
A decision made in a lucid
moment when the legs open
long before the heart.

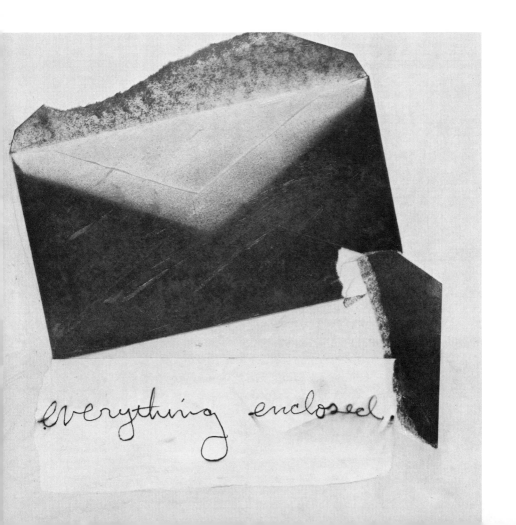

D.C.

There are giant black rats in the dumpster out back.
When the police bust the junkies that hang out in
the alley, they throw them against the dumpster and
yell, "Spread."
Then they open the lid and there is this unearthly
scream and it's the junkie yelling, "Rats! It's
full of rats!" and the police say, "That's right,
motherfucker, now spread."

Today I did a lot. It's Monday. I washed the floor
and table. I swept and killed bugs. I went out and
bought three green apples three peaches three long
pale gladiola. Now they sit in a jar on the table
with a blue scarf wrapped around it. My friend
says I live an immaculate life.

We telephone the young Latin men upstairs.
My friend says, Oigame, listen. Este es
el Man downstairs. Mi casa has water from
su casa. Entiendes? Understand?
And the man says Voy A Ver
I go to see. Soon the water stops.

Besides falling asleep in the bath
these guys fight. They go head over
heals down the stairs, they're thunder
on the hallways. They break furniture
and dishes and teeth. They play records
and slow dance together, a thin layer of
sweat between them and the sobbing song
in the night, all that's left to them of home.

When I come up the street in the day
they motion to me from the windows
and let fall strips of kleenex that
catch in the wind and waver.

The police go by and hit
the sides of the dumpster.
The rats scatter.
They get shot.
I blink, once, then
go on chopping onions.

THE DESCENT OF HEAVEN OVER THE LAKE

Last night swami boiled water in his hands.
Today, from my window, the tree is filled
with blossoms.
I put some in a jar where I sleep and wake
to their reach, the arc and weight of buds,
flowers, all of this in a glass of water.

Sometimes he sits outside all night.
He has stopped his heart and
made it go again. That's what
saddens him each time he
succumbs to the desire to return to the body.

These hyacinths tremble and explode
in the troubled air. Their thin force
spills like a stain against the
unmoving day. I look across the bridge.
I have no heart. The water that I pour
into my hands stays very still.

THE WEIGHT OF DREAMS

The weight of dreams keeps you from raising your head.
Your ear, big as a fetus, curls next to you on the pillow.
It seems to wish for a life of its own. Birth into the arms
of a woman you've never met, innocent of hatred, who has
never laughed at you from a crowd, clutching her husband's
arm, wanting to get away and to look longer, catching your
eye as her own fill with tears, shame, curiosity.

You want to lay in the garden for a few seasons,
until you've assumed that colors of the earth,
your great skull damp, your shining forehead
a catwalk. If only nature could absorb her
mistakes, or forgive them.

You dream that you are handsome and it's snowing.
You hold a child up to the window, and it's like
the two of you are inside a glass ball, a miniature
landscape that you shake and small flakes swirl in water.

But you are captive to a larger sphere; the ridiculous.
You take aimless walks in the rose garden and receive
letters from across the world, the world where others
live with grace, whose foreheads do not swell with sleep
and dreams, stampedes and thunder. The weight of dreams
presses your head farther into the pillow. Your neck
bends like a stem. Your voice rises in thin steam.

You dream that you are a sea trout with a perfect body,
moving with abandon. You dream that your mother never
went to the circus, carrying you inside, taking her
mammoth fright. Was it a dream, lying beneath the
elephants, or simply a condition of the blood.
An affinity for sideshows, tents, the shrieking
baboons lifting their red butts in anger.

As dawn slides over London you imagine a
woman taking off her dress. Gravity
overtakes you, a virgin.

LOSS

You are sitting in the bar in your father's coat.
You have been drinking all weekend, tracing maps
across glasses with a nonchalance that betrays you.
No one is this calm in the face of death.

You keep checking the time in your old man's watch.
Given time, you'll grow into it.
A woman clambers onto the stage
and sings in a ragged voice, ginsoaked.
She is the telling wind behind you.
She says she loves this guy, and
hates him. That he left her. That
it wasn't fair.

Now she sleeps in his pajamas and
a dirty silk housecoat that he forgot.
& she needs another drink & you send
one up to her. She can't see you past
the stagelights, but nods at the dark
in your direction. Halfheartedly you
raise a hand.

III

WHY DO YOU SAY

Why do you say you don love me
'n then pull me down beside
Why do you say you don want me no more
'n then moan like that when I take off
my shirt. Pull me up against you in the alley
'n then say don call me angel no more
'n don speak to me no french.
You put your visage up against my breast
and the moon lies in gutters,
in puddles, but most of all it lies
with me in your arms.
I wait up all night for you with
cigarette burns in my long black night
gown and a heart full of smoke
'n I hear your step on the stair
'n I shake down my hair 'n and put red
on my lips but you too drunk to notice
'n in the morning you don't want me no more
but when you pull me down beside there's nothing else.
'n you lie with me like a birchbark canoe
in the water beneath the trees 'n you whisper
in my neck 'n I don't wash my face for days
'n there's perfume on the rug 'n dirty plates
on the bed and children come
to the windows, peer in, strip away the vines.
I put both my hands in my back pockets
'n they go away.
The stereo is stuck on one song 'n how
it keeps me awake waiting for you.
Finally I tear the cords out of it
'n off the wall 'n the song won't quit
so I lay in bed with the sheets up over
my head 'n they got your smell on em.
Why do you say you don love me no more
n' then moan like that when I take off
my bandages. 'n you stay away so long

'n my heart fills the room with smoke
'n the light hurts my eyes
so I smash out all the bulbs 'n I lie
on the floor 'n the children come,
to the window, peer in, strip the vines from my hair.

FAME / OBSCURITY

The silent
worm on the
mulberry tree
is spinning silk
for parachutes and
kimonas. It draws no
attention to itself
and dies with an
early frost.
A man leaps out of an airplane.
A woman in Kyoto uncovers herself.
We do not question the fabric of
our lives. There is no one to
applaud the small gestures that
we make. The man drifts from the
sky like a kite. The Geisha goes
home alone and when her robe
falls open there is no one to
trace a finger along the
line of her revealed breast.
It's cold, late autumn, she
takes out her pipe, the room
sweetens with the scent of
poppies. She is dreaming
in her chair, the season
forgotten. An ember spills
onto her shellcolor gown
and makes a small burn.
Still, she does not notice.
The lifework of the silkworm
is flawed. The man has finally
landed and tears himself out
of the ropes, leaving what
gentled his flight tangled
in the trees. He walks away slowly,
testing his legs.
Exhilaration succumbs to memory.

COLETTE SAID

It's cruel. Each
reflective dawn
that I have drawn
the shades, keeping
the sun, his gaze,
from falling on my
slackening thighs,
his eyes, in the
shuttered light,
will not discern
the wrinkles and
the lies. I'm aging.
He's a boy.

When he wakes up,
I'm fully dressed,
I'm at my best
covered up, turning
away. He thinks I'm shy.

He has no fear of time,
of lines, or daylight
picking out the places
where my body wearies,
having carried so much
joy, and known
innumerable faces.

I've lost count
of my pleasures.
They've left no
traces, save for
the resonating thrill
that graces, that lives
beneath my skin,
beneath his hands each
time that he erases
all ideas but this;
love in the present tense.

FIRE/WORK/S

On my back at ground zero. They are
mushroom spores that open, hover &
descend directly. They drift down
like extraterrestials, burning as
they fall but when they touch us
we don't feel it. Their colors
turn the night into a red day.
I look at the faces of everyone
and think, "This is what it will
be like when they come. We will
be waiting, sitting on blankets,
families and lovers, we will be
waiting for a bigger life."
The explosions illuminate our position.
We lean expectantly upwards.

STILL LIFE

I awoke in Texas and pulled aside the curtain.
I looked out onto the songless flats and felt
my life grinding to a halt. I let loose of the
drape and thought about places where it snows
for weeks, where the night
is white and lacelike, opening with
dazzling contours like a silent host.

My days are like the narrow dance of a dog
along a fence. Meaning is pulled from beneath me
like a trick with tablecloth and plates.
I have these memories. It's like
licking at pictures of food in magazines.

I never leave my room except to run water
into a glass. Everything is smaller.
Life's old. I sit on a chair in this room
in Texas and appear not to move. Wrong.
In my head the equations are smoking.
I have to count on my fingers.
Father thinks I'm useless, and lazy,
but if I looked away, the numbers
would be sucked like paper boats down
a storm sewer.
That's all. My love to your mama,
if she knows who I am.

TROUT

Row out onto the lake at dawn.
Feel the first mouth. Count
to three. Yank up.

Each time that we let the lines
drop it is like a blind man
who reaches into a black bag,
expecting something from the
unseen. Our faces reflect the
hidden passages of water, the
corridors of reeds and fishes.

We are wearing dopey hats
because we know that these
things matter. Soon teenagers
in a motorboat will roar past,
yelling, and we will hate them
because they are predictable.
Like, much later, as adults,
when they drive north to a
lake and sit rocking in a
wooden boat, looking as dark
and uncomprehending as us, Love.

ILLUSION

The pink
neon made a
halfcircle
on your face
while you slept.
From outside
the flashing
light gave you
a question mark
of a look.
From out the
window pink neon
flashed your face
into a circus of
possible expressions.
Living above the
Waffle Shop has
made you a figure
of mystery.

KANDINSKY, 1910, AFFECTS THE FIRST ABSTRACT

He sees a woman's apron as an expanse
of blue flowers, paints it and goes to bed.
He has turned the picture upside down and
when he awakens does not recognize it.
All color on a field that pleats and ripples.
It means more to him because all meaning is lost.
It scares him. He goes back to drawing small and
tight and representational. He will not be happy
until one day he finds himself back amidst the
abstract. It's everything he's ever wanted, & more.

IV

THE SOUTH DAKOTA POEMS: 1

You live on land in its second year
of drought. Yellow earth, withered stalks.

I come to you speaking shamelessly of water,
reeking chlorine, city pools, a lake. And
I come to you rolling to sleep like a boat,
wet grass on my feet in the morning and
before I came to you I was as thirsty, myself.

By now the corn is tasseled. By now
the pigs are thick with blood. The calves
come up to the fence. I come out from the
house. Wire bristles between us. The dog
darts beneath, he's bored, he eats grass
and thinks about chickens.

I stroll past the flowering crab and
up to the porch. Water stands across
the wood. The radio crackles Rain Tonight
and from the yellow kitchen you call to me,
"It's in the bin. We've made it!"
Not so. For the third year
there's no rain all summer
and the seed blows off with
the maneating wind. By July
you no longer go out to check
the crops and you don't ever
look at the wheat. Your mouth
is a thin line, bitter,
still as a blade.

THE SOUTH DAKOTA POEMS: 2 (BILLY)

When I come out on the porch
you are carrying water back
from the well in your blue shirt
and I vow never to shame you again.
I don't ask about last night, and
you say nothing. You stand in the
light, blinking up at me and wonder
how I'll talk my way out of this one.
It's got to be good, that's half the
reason you keep me here, the stories.

I'm alone out here so long
sometimes it all saves up and
we go into town and I start
in with whiskey and get terrible
and I make you get wild too. But
in the city where I come from no
one would mind. Come inside, I'll
sit on your lap in the kitchen
and teach you dirty songs
the sailors taught me.

Today you'll teach me how to
shoot so tonight we can sit
in bed and take turns picking
off the birds that keep
flying in here
whitening everything.

And when you spike the rye
I squat next to the wheel
on the floor of the tractor
and grip the chain in my fist
and close my eyes and yell,
"It's Africa! It's the sea!"
and you shake your head over
someone so undone by the smell

of wet black earth.

I stared full into the sun.
I see angels behind the henhouse.
This is how I want to die; up here
with you, harvesting the rye,
the dog running in circles around us.

THE SOUTH DAKOTA POEMS: 3

Watch, you warn me,
for the antelope that plunges
from the silky brome grass
along the ditch. & watch,
the cutting scythe explodes
sunflowers into your hands
and boots and pockets. You
are drowning in the cascade
of what you gave and then took
from the earth. I shift, double
clutch, bounce wildly across
the rows with you in the
truckbed swimming in black seeds.

I can almost feel your heart
absorb the grain.
in sleep your head fills with
ripened pods, ready to burst,
promising a yield unheard of
in these parts. These parts.
They call me your boy. You
laugh it off, running your
hand along my willfull skull.
Watch your fingers for the
blade, watch the sky for moisture,
never curse the earth.

When snow drifts seven feet
and smothers the weakest calves,
when snow drifts through the
kitchen and across the table,
rest your head in your arms
and I will come from the city
like a dream, whispering visions
of an early thaw into your dusty hair
against sheets that smell of grain.

68

THE SOUTH DAKOTA POEMS: 4

How it was that my life moved so far
from yours I cannot say. The trees
were bursting open. I took to hanging
out the window in my boredom.
The moon made a stain on the rug.

The Canadian geese head
north over the house.
Last year I would've
run out and made you
come call them with me.
This year you hear them
from the kitchen and do not move.

Tonight the snow glitters.
I stumble to the back bedroom.
Where you are, the dog jumps a
fence and bloodies sheep.
My mouth shines from purple
lipstick. The dog's eyes glitter
from behind the legs of yet
another lamb.

You have to beat him
and ask yourself, Is
there no end to this?
And I, poised and trembling,
wonder the same. I pull on
a white kimona and stare
into an empty glass.
Where you are the radiant
crabtree dies.
You replace it with a
flowering lotus.

THE SOUTH DAKOTA POEMS: 5

(SELLING GRAIN TO RUSSIA)

Soon you will be loading it onto trucks.
Then ships, all the days of our summers
all the dreams of wheat and the desire
for rain. What waved and rippled on all
sides of us, what was the world, floats
now toward Moscow. You can buy a
car and fix the roof. The land around
you waits chastely for winter. You retreat
into the house.

Men have been speaking through
interpreters, making tentative
steps towards coexistance, the
balance of bread against missiles,
the golden heads of grain that lay
shoveled into mountains, whole
countrysides of sweet rising loaves
exchanged for a thin promise;
bakeries instead of bombs.

For you a roof that doesn't leak.
Maybe a bathroom indoors.
Something to show for.
To compensate for the grit
embedded in your face, your
neck burned red forever,
a reason for the early aging,
your battered hands, the rough
and angry language of a
disappointed man. Every day
you fight the sun, breathe dirt,
worst of all you wait, and wait
for the cycle of life to come
around again.

I dream simple things about you.
Handing you a glass of water.
Taking off your boots. Unfurling
a blanket across the bed. These
memories of thirst have put you
in my mind again. You're looking
swell. You penetrate this swamp,
interrupt the shoreline, waver
in the distance down along the
beach. A rainforest. The jungle.
I think of you, my lips parch.

My eyes grow red with salt. I think of you.
The insomnia of drought.
The unblinking eye of the sun.
The comatose earth, settling
deeper into the sleep that
approaches death. You stand
in a cracked field, licking
your mouth, the only stalk, upright,
from here to the horizon.

IN SOUTH DAKOTA THERE IS A WORD

In South Dakota there is a word for Hail. The white
combine that drives in the dark and goes against

Nature. "Eight hundred acres," you say over the phone,
"It's like all my friends are waving goodbye from a boat."

"I'm standing on shore waving my ticket. This is the
year I was supposed to make it. Instead I crawled beneath

my tractor and watched the hail take my crop."

When the stalks are damaged the heads of the sunflowers
keep filling while their own weight wrestles them down

to the ground. You watch for slow weeks and when all
their faces are in the mud you decide to go into town.

The sky froze and turned white and cracked and fell down.

THE REAL STORY OF FRANK

There is a girl by the river
in a red cotton dress. Two guys
strike up a fire in a cave.
The monster stirs. Fear of flame enlarges
his heart until it shatters the cage of ice.
His unrequited love is loosed on the world,
which can't take it. He lurches forward, no
more successful and with no more luck than
any thawed compulsion gets. The villagers
pick up clubs and give chase.

The girl is afraid for herself
and for the thing. Why does he
find her beautiful? Why did he find her at all?
To shield him with her small body would be impossible.
He turns his head and his mismatched nostrils flare at
the smell of fire again. The mob is upon them. She takes
him in her arms like a lover. No one stops.
They stampede past. She points him towards
the road. My darling, the danger is over.
It will never be so good for us again.
Go away, sweetheart, before I start screaming.

V

DNA

Inside the cell sliced with a razor
a world peels away and leafs onto
the lens. It will be frozen, and
photographed, and enlarged.
We say, "helix," and hold the
word in our mouths.
There is a baroque swirl
whose curl is a code.

The calligrapher's brush is poised
above the circle it will make
in one stroke. We would say the
circle is empty. Look closer,
its tendrils are entwining.
The very movement of life
climbs in front of itself,
then behind, then in front,
and so on.

GANGES

In this night
of no small
drunkenness
we pass like
men in a boat,
men laughing
from the back
of a truck, dizzy
with the wanton spin
of the world.
In this night
drunkenness is
a holy river,
soiled and sainted.
We dip in, dusty
pilgrims, no longer
expecting miracles,
content simply
to rise
to the surface
again.

PICKERS

On the 4th day
of gin and motorcycles
we stopped somewhere
north of Laredo and
went into the first
doorway that spilled
dark, and cool, and jukey.
My back was worn raw from
the holes in the road
that I took with my ass
instead of my feet.
These exhausted cowboy
boots twitched electric
up and down my spine.
You were going to
find a job in Texas
but only looked from
the end of an uplifted glass.
All you could see was me,
and the road stretching out
like a cat who is ready to run.
Manana, you said, and I
pictured the tatoos on
your arms glistening
with sweat as you
leaned over another
bushel of tomatoes.
A picker. Migrant.
All that remains
is the grease spot
on a borrowed mattress.
Manana, I decided, means
never. The heat pushed
from behind us like
an iron and bound
us together in a

tight packet of misery,
stuck to each other and
each other's ways with
only a thin film of sweat between us.
You own yourself
when no one else
will have you.

LABUZATIE: A BURIAL IN THE GARDEN

With spring comes
the hyacinth and
covers the little
black grave.
There will be small
blue flowers, & later,
with summer, roses.
The earth is his nurse.
His memory is slowly
becoming part of the garden.

Now I walk in the wet snow
and my heart is bitter.
As I say to my wife, "So
be it." She nods and goes
on spreading the last of
the grapes on newspaper.
They'll sweeten, and
shrivel, and late autumn
we'll drink wine, the
rarified air of this
season, and smile through
the lens of the glass.

Words will return to her,
as time muffles our loss.
And desire, too, will
assume its rightful place.
And the goat will get a
little goat, and the rabbits
and ducks will need to be fed.
Nothing so wild and mysterious
as the cackling hen, filled
with an animal joy, unable
to imagine any life but this.

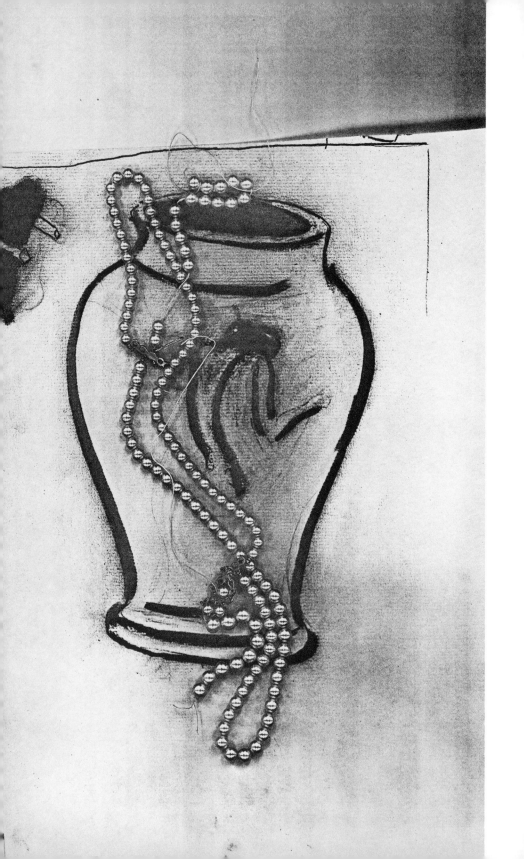

THE SPINE OF PEARL

Hiroko in the bath
consents to have her
back washed. I take
up the long wooden
brush and the sea sponge,
she ties up her black hair
and leans forward. The
skin becomes pink beneath
my efforts, the water
milky, the color of pearl.
She sighs and closes her eyes.
I am falling in love with
her spine, the line where
the gentle swell of breast begins.
Mother is asleep.
I want to tumble fully clothed
into the bath. I want to
embrace Hiroko and yet not
touch her, surround her like
the little waves that slide
back away as she rises.
I hand her the towel.
A cloud of talcum
mingles with the steam
and obscures the mirror.
I am dying to touch the mole
on her shoulder with my mouth.

At mother's funeral
Hiroko told me gay
stories about Japan.
She said no one ever
accepts food from
another's chopstick
with her own because
in an ancient custom
the bone chips of the
incinerated dead are
passed that way,
through each member
of the family and then
into an urn.
She left to visit a man
who brought strawberries
in the dead of winter,
and champagne. A man
whose poems always
mentioned the passing
season. Our guests
were shocked. She laughed
from behind her perfect hand,
even smaller than mine. I was huge
and clumsy walking her to the car.

It was from her that I first
tasted sushi, pink and raw,
and from her I learned of
the search for the ox,
how to capture the unknown,
tame it,
then let it go,
replacing desire
with the single stroke
of a circle,
empty, complete.

LI PO

Last night we watched the moon
move behind a cloud.
In the river I saw Li Po
embracing history. He looked
profoundly stoned.

Since then I hear that
he drowned. I also hear
that his widow goes
down to the spot
and watches the sky
from the arms of the
boatman.

Li Po's perfect
desire swims now
with the little
fishes. He wears
a lily pad for his hat.

THE MINNESOTA VOICES PROJECT

1981

1   Deborah Keenan, HOUSEHOLD WOUNDS (poems), $3.00

2   John Minczeski, THE RECONSTRUCTION OF LIGHT (poems), $3.00

The First Annual Competition

3   John Solensten, THE HERON DANCER (stories), $5.00

4   Madelon Sprengnether Gohlke, THE NORMAL HEART (poems), $3.00

5   Ruth Roston, I LIVE IN THE WATCHMAKERS' TOWN (poems), $3.00

6   Laurie Taylor, CHANGING THE PAST (poems), $3.00

1982

7   Alvaro Cardona-Hine, WHEN I WAS A FATHER (a poetic memoir), $4.00

The Second Annual Competition

8   Richard Broderick, NIGHT SALE (stories), $5.00

9   Katherine Carlson, CASUALTIES (stories), $5.00

#10   Sharon Chmielarz, DIFFERENT ARRANGEMENTS (poems), $3.00

#11   Yvette Nelson, WE'LL COME WHEN IT RAINS (poems), $3.00

1983

#12   Madelon Sprengnether, RIVERS, STORIES, HOUSES, DREAMS (familiar essays,) $4.00

#13   Wendy Parrish, BLENHEIM PALACE (poems), $3.00

The Third Annual Competition

#14   Perry Glasser, SUSPICIOUS ORIGINS (short stories), $6.00

#15   Marisha Chamberlain, POWERS (poems), $3.50

#16   Michael Moos, MORNING WINDOWS (poems), $3.50

#17   Mark Vinz, THE WEIRD KID (prose poems), $3.50

#18   Neal Bowers, THE GOLF BALL DIVER (poems), $3.50

Jonis Agee, and others, eds. BORDER CROSSINGS: A MINNESOTA VOICES
   PROJECT READER, $8.00

The Fourth Annual Competition

#19   Margaret Hasse, STARS ABOVE, STARS BELOW (poems), $3.50

#20   C. J. Hribal, MATTY'S HEART (short stories) $6.00

#21   Sheryle Noethe, THE DESCENT OF HEAVEN OVER THE LAKE
   (poems), $3.50

#22   Monica Ochtrup, WHAT I CANNOT SAY/I WILL SAY (poems) $3.50

*Copies of any or all of these books may be purchased directly from the publisher
by filling out the coupons below and mailing it, together with a check for the cor-
rect amount and $1.00 per order for postage and handling, to:*

New Rivers Press
1602 Selby Ave.
St. Paul, MN 55104

_____

Please send me the following books: _____

_____

_____

_____

_____

_____

I am enclosing $_____ (which includes $1.00 for postage and handling)
Please send these books as soon as possible to:

   NAME _____

   ADDRESS _____

   CITY & STATE _____

   ZIP _____